Mighty Machines
TRUCKS

Jean Coppendale

Firefly Books

A FIREFLY BOOK

Published by Firefly Books Ltd. 2010

First printing

Publisher Cataloging-in-Publication Data (U.S.)

Coppendale, Jean.
   Trucks : mighty machines / Jean Coppendale.
[24] p. : col. photos. ; cm.
Includes index.
Summary: A fun book about trucks for young readers, including dump trucks, snow trucks and transporters.
ISBN-13: 978-1-55407-619-2 (pbk.)
ISBN-10: 1-55407-619-6 (pbk.)
1. Trucks – Juvenile literature.   2. Dump trucks – Juvenile literature. I. Title.
[E]   629.224 dc22   TL230.15C677 2010

A CIP record for this book is available from Library and Archives Canada

Published in the United States by
Firefly Books (U.S.) Inc.
P.O. Box 1338, Ellicott Station
Buffalo, New York 14205

Published in Canada by
Firefly Books Ltd.
66 Leek Crescent
Richmond Hill, Ontario L4B 1H1

Manufactured by 1010 Printing International Ltd. in Huizhou, Guangdong, China in December 2009, Job #JQ09100342.

Author Jean Coppendale
Designer Rahul Dhiman (Q2A Media)
Editor Katie Bainbridge
Picture Researcher Lalit Dalal (Q2A Media)

Publisher Steve Evans
Creative Director Zeta Davies
Senior Editor Hannah Ray

Words in **bold** can be found in the glossary on page 23.

Contents

What is a truck?

Trucks are used to carry things from one place to another. They also help us build homes, roads and bridges. Some trucks are the size of a car, others can be as big as a house.

At the front of a truck is a cab where the driver sits. The back of a truck is called a bed or trailer.

cab **trailer**

A trailer is hooked to a cab.

5

Transporters

Big trucks that are used to carry very heavy loads are called transporters.

Some transporters carry the heaviest load you can imagine, such as boats and even space shuttles.

This transporter is pulling a space shuttle to its **launchpad**.

Some transporters have long, strong trailers called flatbeds. The load sits on top of the flatbed. Other transporters have a big box instead, and the load is carried inside the box.

A car transporter takes new cars to the showroom.

flatbed

Long trucks

Long trucks, called **tandem-trailer trucks**, carry loads over very long distances. Some drivers spend months on the road, so their trucks have beds, refrigerators, toilets and even televisions inside.

Tandem-trailer trucks pull huge trailers. Each trailer can be as long as ten cars lined up in a row.

Each trailer has several sets of chunky wheels.

Logging trucks

When trees are cut down, trucks called loggers are used to carry the logs to the **timber mills**.

A stack of logs is loaded onto the long trailer behind the logging truck's cab.

Loggers often have to travel long distances to timber mills.

Dump trucks

Some of the world's biggest trucks are dump trucks. These trucks are used to move earth and rocks where **mines** are being dug.

Dump trucks have huge wheels, more than three times taller than you.

This dump truck is emptying its load backward. With some dump trucks, no one has to do any **manual** unloading.

Smaller dump trucks are used on **construction sites**. The back of the truck tips up so that the load slides off.

On the building site

Many different types of trucks are used on construction sites. **Concrete** mixers mix cement, sand and water together to make concrete. The concrete is then poured down a pipe or **chute**, ready to use.

drum

Concrete mixers have a drum on the back that spins around and around to keep the concrete smooth.

This man is using a remote control to move the crane on the truck.

Crane trucks have strong mechanical arms called cranes. They can pick up and move heavy bags of gravel or sand.

Clean streets

Trucks are used for everyday jobs, such as keeping our streets clean and collecting garbage. Street cleaners are small trucks with water hoses and brushes. They wash the street and sweep up small bits of garbage.

Street cleaners are small trucks operated by one person.

This garbage truck has an arm which picks up the trash can, empties it, and then puts it down.

Big garbage trucks empty trash cans for us. They take the garbage to special sites where it is buried or **recycled**.

Snow trucks

Trucks can be used for clearing snow. Snowblowers blow snow away through a chute. They are used for clearing roads and runways at airports.

Snowplows make sure the roads are clear so that
cars can keep moving and not get stuck in the snow.

This snowblower has chains on its wheels. They stop it from slipping on the snow and ice.

Snowplows have a shovel or plow on the front. This pushes the snow out of the way and clears the road.

Meet **Bigfoot**

Monster trucks are specially built for shows and competitions. They are ordinary trucks with giant wheels and big engines.

The biggest and heaviest monster truck in the world is called Bigfoot 5.

Monster trucks compete in events such as mud racing, jumping in the air and crushing vehicles.

The trucks are often painted with bright colors and have flames, stripes or pictures on the sides and **hood**.

Activities

- Make a truck collection. Collect pictures of trucks from magazines. Put them in size order starting with the biggest truck, or group them by what they do.

- What do these trucks do?

- Draw your own truck. Where is it going? What is it carrying? Write a short story to go with it.

- Can you name these parts of a truck?

- Have you seen a truck today? What color was it? Do you know what kind of truck it was?

Glossary

Chute
The pipe through which some material is poured in or out of a truck.

Concrete
A building material that is made up of cement, water and either gravel or sand.

Construction sites
Areas of land where buildings, such as houses or offices, are built.

Hood
The metal lid covering the engine at the front of a truck or car. The driver lifts the hood to look at the engine, battery and other mechanical parts that make the truck or car move.

Launchpad
The place where a space shuttle begins its journey.

Manual
A process carried out by hand.

Mines
Places where things such as coal or gold are dug out of the ground.

Recycled
When garbage is changed into something new and is reused.

Tandem-trailer trucks
Really big, long trucks that can pull up to six trailers.

Timber mills
A place where large logs are cut into smaller pieces.

Index